Faith Questions
Suffering

KYRA DANIELS

nature & essence

What is *Suffering?*

Suffering is a state of sorrow, distress, or pain. In the midst of suffering, we experience internal grief that is felt within our souls. Our hearts ache and mourn during the state of suffering and cause us to look at what is wrong. We are quick to identify our experiences of suffering as bad, wrong, or evil. We do not want to remain in our suffering but want to move toward healing and relief.

Suffering can also be described as hardship under harsh rule. In this context, a relationship causes our suffering—an oppressor evokes pain, and we as the oppressed experience pain. Control characterizes this type of suffering. We find ourselves in bondage, encountering abuse and exploitation at the hands of a brutal tyrant. This affliction is cruel and unjust treatment. Suffering like this involves unjustifiable pain that cries for freedom and justice.

Dan McCartney, in his book, *Why Does It Have to Hurt: The Meaning of Christian Suffering*, also defines suffering as "alienation." Alienation is the state of isolation and separation from the group to which one belongs. Again, this suffering involves a relationship, but more specifically, the brokenness of such a relationship. McCartney claims that suffering is alienation from others, self, or God. This brokenness manifests itself in feelings we have of abandonment, betrayal, depression, humiliation, and hopelessness. When we experience this type of suffering, we seek reconciliation and wholeness.

SUFFERING IS A STATE OF SORROW,
DISTRESS, OR PAIN.

6

What is the *Origin* of Suffering?

The Bible, which is the Word of God, provides the origin of suffering in the world. In the book of Genesis, the author wrote a narrative account of creation and the fall of man. Under the guidance of the Holy Spirit, he rightly depicted God as the benevolent Creator of the universe. God was present before the foundation of the world, and there was no other god like Him. By His very words, God formed the sky and sea. His divine speech created landscape, vegetation, animals, and humans in their maturity. God blessed His work, and so all of the creation flourished in His loving presence. Man and woman, Adam and Eve lived in harmony with each other, with nature, and with God. In relationship with their Creator, Adam and Eve experienced fullness and joy in the garden of Eden. They dealt with no suffering or pain. Scripture tells us that God's intention for His creation was abundance and life. This design was the reality at the beginning, but it took an awful turn in Genesis 3.

God graciously gave Adam and Eve, our first parents, paradise, but they chose to follow their own desires instead. In the garden, a spiritual evil was present, seeking to distort the words of God and bring destruction to His beautiful creation. Satan, disguised as a serpent, tempted Adam and Eve to eat from the tree God forbade. Presented with the opportunity, Adam and Eve sinned against God. To sin means to fall short of God's divine law. Their disobedience made spiritual evil their lord and ushered in suffering of all kinds. Mirroring the alienation McCartney describes, the man and woman felt shame and hid from each other and God. Their personal sin permeated the world and brought death and curse. Adam and Eve were exiled from the garden, and their relationship with God and satisfaction in His presence were gone. There was total disharmony and brokenness. Sin introduced suffering, and the mourning began over all that was lost and corrupted.

"
GOD GRACIOUSLY GAVE ADAM AND EVE, OUR FIRST PARENTS, PARADISE, BUT THEY CHOSE TO FOLLOW THEIR OWN DESIRES INSTEAD.

Is Suffering *Real?*

Because of its biblical framework, Christianity recognizes the origin of suffering as the result of evil and sin. However, the non-Christian worldview does not have such a rational explanation for the presence of suffering. Some worldviews perceive suffering as an illusion. According to these viewpoints, if God is not real, then evil and suffering cannot be real. Instead, suffering is the result of chemical activity in the brain and nervous system, making us label an experience as such. These viewpoints provide that there is no One God who is concerned about His people's hardship. Good and evil do not exist, and there is no purpose or design. Instead, the system of laws operating in the universe—nature—is random, blind, and apathetic. Nature allows any event to occur, and we are thrown around and shaken at its whim. And, because of our advanced cognitive faculties, we imagine this as suffering rather than simply pointless, natural activity.

But, this argument is not satisfying. You cannot tell a child suffering from cancer that pain is an illusion. Christians understand that suffering is a reality and a part of our fallen world. God grieves over this pain and desires better for His creation.

the reach of suffering

How is Suffering
Manifested?

The effect of Adam and Eve's sin permeated the world. As a result, the natural inclination to sin became a part of our humanity. Thoroughly depraved, we are sinners at our core. We are all guilty of crimes against the just God. Romans 3:23 states, "For all have sinned and fall short of the glory of God." Sin had a cosmic effect, causing all of creation to fall from God's original design. As the curse of disobedience spread, suffering spread as well, and death would manifest in all areas of life. Genesis 3:16-19 introduces how suffering would be a part of the human experience because of our own rebellion against God and the fallen world in which we live.

First, the joyous creativity of having children is tainted by intense pain and disappointment. Women suffer from excruciating labor, miscarriages, and stillbirths. Some mothers develop resentment toward the children they birthed in pain—seeing them no longer as gifts but as burdens. Children are naturally rebellious and disobedient, many developing a dishonor and hatred toward their parents. Within families, there may be jealousy, rivalry, and favoritism. Familial conflicts grow into conflicts with neighbors, and these conflicts grow into war and prejudice.

Second, hostility exists between men and women. Marriages face infidelity, deceit, abuse, and divorce. God-given gender distinctions are not celebrated. Viewing the other as too difficult to love, men and women forsake one another, pursuing their own image instead. Competition plays out at home and in the workplace. Both sides take advantage and manipulate, striving to maintain their power dynamics.

Finally, work and nature are distorted. The earth is cursed. There are earthquakes, hurricanes, and other natural disasters that wipe out people and places. Work is harsh and futile, people struggle with purpose and weakness, and physical death is inevitable. Eventually, our time will come to an end, and we will be forgotten. As we encounter sickness and disease, we are reminded of our limitations and frailty in each day that passes.

Stories of

Grief

"Death seemed like a stranger until my grandmother passed away. In September, I traveled to Kentucky for her funeral. Imogene laid peacefully in the casket. She was dressed beautifully in her favorite mahogany outfit and pearl jewelry. I admired her and cried, remembering her life as the matriarch of the family. This should not be. I thought. The grief sent my body into a 'flight or fight' response: I began to overheat and sweat. My mouth turned dry. I froze like prey when a dangerous predator is present. Death stood beside me like an uninvited visitor as I looked at my grandmother."

KYRA RILEY, "HOPE IN SORROWFUL SEASONS"
blog post for The Daily Grace Co.

"I'll never forget the moment she caught me. My body went into shock. The online sexual sin was exposed, and I could no longer live in the shadows. The relationship was over, and it was a messy split. In the midst of it all, I was asked not to come back to church for a while. In addition, the moment she caught me triggered the sexual abuse of my past. I was trying to heal from two heartbreaks at the same time. I had nothing but Jesus—which was everything I had needed for so long. Through God's severe mercy, I was broken, but through it, I learned life could be more full than I ever imagined."

ANONYMOUS SUBMISSION

"The elders of Daughter Zion
sit on the ground in silence.
They have thrown dust on their heads
and put on sackcloth.
The young women of Jerusalem
have bowed their heads to the ground.
My eyes are worn out from weeping;
I am churning within.
My heart is poured out in grief
because of the destruction of my dear people,
because infants and nursing babies faint
in the streets of the city."

LAMENTATIONS 2:10-11

the accusation against God

Suffering and
God's Power

Many of us struggle with the idea that while God is all-powerful, suffering and evil still exist. And some of us, though we believe in God, are unable to reconcile this tension, and therefore, we limit His divine attributes. We believe that God must not be omnipotent. For others of us, this tension leads to denying God's existence entirely. But, though there is a mystery between the existence of suffering and the power of God, there is not a contradiction. A contradiction implies that there are two statements or ideas opposed to each other. For example, someone holds the two following statements to be true: "The moon is made entirely of cheese" and "The moon is not made entirely of cheese." These two supposed truths bring a contradiction because one idea denies the other. And therefore, one or both statements must be false. Now, compare another two statements: "God is all-powerful" and "Suffering exists." The fact that suffering exists does not deny the power of God. God's power is an independent attribute. An independent attribute means that its reality does not rely on anything else for it to be true. The omnipotence of God remains undiminished, even while suffering is present. Daniel 3:17-18 states, "If the God we serve exists, then he can rescue us from the furnace of blazing fire, and he can rescue us from the power of you, the king. But even if he does not rescue us, we want you as king to know that we will not serve your gods or worship the gold statue you set up." The prophet Daniel was threatened with murder when he did not bow to Nebuchadnezzar and the gods of Babylon, but Daniel knew that God was powerful enough to save him and his friends from death. Daniel also knew that if the Lord chose not to, the truth of His power could not be tarnished. Through Scripture, we see that even when God does not provide relief, we can trust that He is able. We can hold on to the Lord's unshakeable strength to give us courage in hardship, for evil cannot destroy God's power.

Suffering and
God's Presence

We may wonder whether or not God is present with us through suffering. When experiencing loss, abuse, or death, we question if God sees us and is near. Suffering evokes a longing for comfort and empathy, and when we as sufferers feel isolated, alone, or misunderstood, it is easy to cast doubt on God's presence. When we limit God's presence in times of suffering, we are holding to the idea of deism, the belief that God does not intervene in the universe—that He is a creator who has taken His hands off of creation to allow the natural events bringing about good, evil, and suffering to run their course. The deistic god does not desire to be with His people when they are going through hard times.

However, the deistic god is not the true God of the universe. Scripture shows us that God not only sees and is moved to compassion when we as His people are suffering, but He is also moved to be with us in suffering. In Exodus 3:7-8, God says to Moses, "I have observed the misery of my people in Egypt, and have heard them crying out because of their oppressors. I know about their sufferings, and I have come down to rescue them from the power of the Egyptians and to bring them from that land to a good and spacious land, a land flowing with milk and honey…" At this point in redemptive history, God saw the pain of slavery the Israelites faced, assured them with His words of promise, and came down to rescue them. Because He is omnipresent — everywhere at all times — the Spirit of God was present with the Israelites from slavery to temple. And God continues to be with His people through trials today. Through the indwelling Holy Spirit, the soothing presence of God is always near and comforts us in the midst of the darkness.

WHEN WE LIMIT GOD'S PRESENCE IN TIMES OF
SUFFERING, WE ARE HOLDING TO THE IDEA
OF DEISM, THE BELIEF THAT GOD DOES NOT
INTERVENE IN THE UNIVERSE...

Suffering and
God's Sovereignty

What does it mean that God is sovereign? Sovereignty speaks of God's control over everything that happens. God reigns as King of kings. He has power and authority over all, and therefore, He has influence over everything that happens. Nothing can come to pass without God ordaining or decreeing it. But does this mean that God ordains suffering? God is not the author of evil. In other words, He does not sin or cause bad things to occur. Bad things occur because of sin, spiritual evil, and the fallen condition of the world. But, the workings of sin and evil do not occur outside of the hand of God. So, God in his sovereignty has active control over the suffering we experience. But, because He is good, God directly uses it for His redemptive purposes. This mysterious activity is called "concurrence," which means that two or more parties can act in the same event to produce an outcome with different intentions. In this way, God's divine activity runs parallel to the activity of people or spiritual evil, but God always has a good intention to preserve His glory and redeem His people. In Genesis 50:20, Joseph, who had been sold into slavery by his brothers, states, "You planned evil against me; God planned it for good to bring about the present result—the survival of many people." Through Joseph's suffering, his brothers exercised hatred and wanted to dehumanize him by making him a foreign slave. Through Joseph's suffering, Satan wanted to tempt the Israelites away from God and His promises. But, praise be to God, through Joseph's suffering, God put him in a place of influence in Egypt and saved the Israelites from famine, continuing His redemptive mission. From Scripture, we can know that even when we are enduring hardship, God is in control and working everything for good.

PART FOUR

false

hope

$\mathscr{Self}$ as Savior

Non-Christians seek other explanations for the presence of suffering. Many who recognize the existence of a higher being but deny the reality of one true God for all have joined the New Age movement. New Age philosophy is a common worldview in our culture today. Marked by positive and progressive thinking, it teaches that evil and suffering exist because our minds will them to exist. If this were true, it would mean that our suffering is only an illusion. And if suffering was simply a product of our wills and not real, we could overcome it the same way — by willing it away through the power of our minds. Our positivity and perseverance could reverse the negative state that leads to suffering. New Age believers focus on separating the mind from the body, essentially ignoring the presence of suffering and pain in the physical world. Using meditation, mantras, and out-of-body experiences, New Agers seek a higher consciousness to transcend all that is associated with this life. They aim to loosen their grip on identities, materials, and honors that would define us because they believe that in these definitions and earthly pursuits, there is suffering. Instead, New Agers look within themselves to be their own saviors from the suffering world. But, they fail to realize that they are sinful humans and do not possess the enlightened attitude and moral vigor to save themselves. New Age philosophy is reminiscent of the Gnosticism that seeped into the early church. Similar to New Age, Gnosticism rejected matter and materials and claimed that only the spirit was essential and good. Gnostics in the early church argued that Christ did not resurrect in His own flesh but took on spiritual form. But, in Genesis 1, Scripture affirms the goodness of the material world. Furthermore, Scripture speaks of Jesus's physical resurrection and His second coming in the flesh. 2 John 7 claims that all who reject the physical resurrection are deceivers. In its rejection of the physically-resurrected Jesus, New Age philosophy is a lie, putting false hope in oneself.

NEW AGERS LOOK WITHIN THEMSELVES TO BE THEIR OWN SAVIORS FROM THE SUFFERING WORLD. BUT, THEY FAIL TO REALIZE THAT THEY ARE SINFUL HUMANS AND DO NOT POSSESS THE ENLIGHTENED ATTITUDE AND MORAL VIGOR TO SAVE THEMSELVES.

Pleasures as Relief

The opposite of New Age transcendentalism is materialism. Proponents of the materialist worldview believe that suffering is the result of social injustices and economic inequities. Materialists deny the existence or lessen the importance of spirituality and instead focus only on the physical and natural. To overcome suffering, they seek to address any lack in the social, economic, or political sphere. In other words, a materialist would pursue pleasure, wealth, and power to achieve higher satisfaction in life. For example, a Wall Street stock trader works endless hours to be the top and most influential in the field. A college student engages in casual sex to satisfy his lustful appetite. A gambler cannot stop her rounds at the casino until she has achieved the desired amount to fill her financial void. In the materialism philosophy, one seeks an indulgence in the things of this world for the relief of suffering. However, these indulgences are idols and will only lead to destruction. In the end, the pursuit of materialism will lead to an abandoning of ethics and push us further away from God and others. Money, wealth, and power are not meant to satisfy the deeper longing of our souls.

While the materialist philosophy is right to fight against social inequalities that bring about suffering, it is wrong to seek salvation through materialism. The alleviation of poverty and the increase of wealth will not numb the spiritual suffering that sin brings; they will not reconcile the chasm between us and God. The enjoyment of pleasures like food, sex, and relationships will not truly fulfill, but they are meant to point to the ultimate fulfillment found only in God. Like New Age transcendentalism, materialism places false hope in idols that cannot deliver. In 1 Corinthians 10:14, Scripture commands us to "flee from idolatry" because God is jealous for His people. He is passionately concerned about the welfare of His children and wants to bless them with the only thing that can provide relief in suffering: Himself.

"IN THE END,
THE PURSUIT OF
MATERIALISM WILL
LEAD TO AN
ABANDONING OF ETHICS
AND PUSH US FURTHER
AWAY FROM GOD
AND OTHERS."

*the need
for God*

The Reality
of God

Despite the various worldviews of our culture, none of them offer a rational explanation and resolution for the presence of suffering. Nonbelievers may attempt to lean on intellect, inner strength, moral behavior, and privilege to overcome suffering, but Scripture is clear that our good works are not effective. Isaiah 64:6 states, "All of us have become like something unclean, and all our righteous acts are like a polluted garment; all of us wither like a leaf, and our iniquities carry us away like the wind." We cannot rely on ourselves to surpass sin, evil, and suffering. Instead, we must lean on God. In Jeremiah 9:24, God says, "But the one who boasts should boast in this: that he understands and knows me — that I am the Lord, showing faithful love, justice, and righteousness on the earth, for I delight in these things." Suffering is real, but so is God. The fact that we have an understanding of pure wickedness and evil proves that we instinctively know that pure goodness and righteousness exist. The fact that we know to reject oppression, pain, and hardship in all forms proves that we know to seek the true source of justice, peace, and satisfaction. God must be real in order to define what suffering is. The presence of suffering shows the reality of an all-good and loving God and the reality of comfort and joy before Him. There is no suffering is in His presence. God is not like us and the idols we seek. Unmatched, He is perfect, holy, and more than capable of defeating sin and suffering in His world.

WE CANNOT RELY ON OURSELVES TO
SURPASS SIN, EVIL, AND SUFFERING.
INSTEAD, WE MUST LEAN ON GOD.

God's Plan of
Redemption, Restoration, and Healing

Unlike the God of deism who simply watches suffering unfold, the true God not only exists and is concerned about the catastrophe of evil, but He is also actively working against it. God is also not reactive to suffering. In other words, He was not prompted to come up with a solution in response to evil. Instead, the eternal God knew in eternity past what He would do to redeem His creation. Before the foundation of the world, God had a plan to save His people from sin and its effects. This plan made its first appearance in Genesis 3:15, which states, "I will put hostility between you and the woman, and between your offspring and her offspring. He will strike your head, and you will strike his heel." In speaking to the serpent—Satan—who had tempted Adam and Eve in the garden of Eden, the Lord predicted that a Son would come to defeat evil. Through ending the power of sin and evil, this Son would return God's world to the glory of Eden in a new creation. The Promised Son would reverse the curse and the reach of suffering.

Throughout biblical history, God continued to unfold this promise through His covenant relationship with the Israelites, His chosen people. Through them, God made known His character and redemptive plan, which was to free His people from the power of sin and restore them to rest and right worship in His presence. Furthermore, through the Israelites, He would bring this anointed Son—the Savior and Redeemer. The perfect and righteous Son would be the eternal Son of God Himself, who created the world with the Father and Holy Spirit. Through Him, God would forgive sin, cleanse His people, and heal them from the pain of suffering. And, by His life-giving Spirit, He will make it possible through His second coming for them to live in His presence with complete delight, joy, and satisfaction. All who have faith in Jesus, both Jews and Gentiles, become part of God's people. And though sin and suffering will continue on this side of heaven, Christ's death and resurrection ensured that His people—believers—will one day be raised up with new, heavenly bodies to spend eternity with Him in heaven—sin and evil, pain and sadness, buried in the grave.

The *War* against Sin, Suffering, and Evil

The war-like language of Genesis 3:15 helps us understand the tension between God's redemptive plan and the scheme of evil. First, God spoke of hostility between Satan and the offspring of Eve. 1 Peter 5:8 tells us that Satan is a "roaring lion" searching for his next victim. He is a thief who wants to steal, kill, and destroy God's creation (John 10:10). Satan wants us to suffer in this world, and more importantly, he wants suffering to pull us away from God and the life He desires for us. Ephesians 6:12 states, "For our struggle is not against flesh and blood, but against the rulers, against the authorities, against the cosmic powers of this darkness, against evil, spiritual forces in the heavens." There is a spiritual enemy who has rebelled against God with his kingdom of darkness. But, God has waged war on this enemy. In the next part of Genesis 3:15, God pronounced hostility between the Promised Son and Satan. The Son of God would come not only as the Redeemer but also as King and the commander of heaven's army. His sorrow over the suffering in the world would move Him to the divine defense of God's kingdom. Through God's redemptive plan, the Son would fight the battle for us, and though His heel would be bruised by the serpent, He would fully defeat the kingdom of evil. Until the Son's coming, Scripture highlights the tension between God's kingdom and the kingdom of darkness. Throughout redemptive history in the Bible, we can see the war continuing to rage. But, even in such suffering, the people of God remained expectant of the coming Savior and looked to God for strength.

PART SIX

*victory
and comfort
in Christ*

Christ as Chief Sufferer

So often, suffering can feel lonely and isolating. We can feel as if we are alone in our pain, trapped and unable to get out. Yet, we are not alone. The Lord is with us in every trial; through every moment of suffering, He carries us. And even more, He knows and understands our suffering because He too experienced the utmost degree of suffering—death on a cross and, in that, separation from God. Receiving the commission from the Father to redeem the world and defeat evil through His death and resurrection, the eternal Son came to earth. He descended from His heavenly throne and entered history. God became a man. Not compromising His deity or divine attributes, the anointed Son took on flesh and was named Jesus. He came into the world as we all do—through the pain and suffering of labor. Even at His birth, Jesus already felt the weight of sin, and as He grew, He saw more and more the effects of sin's curse on the world.

Jesus was moved with empathy and sorrow for the fallen condition of His creation. Matthew 9:36 states, "When he saw the crowds, he felt compassion for them, because they were distressed and dejected, like sheep without a shepherd." During His ministry, Jesus sought those who were suffering and liberated them from sin's power. He healed the sick, fed the hungry, cast out demons, and raised the dead. Jesus preached that God's kingdom was near. In other words, with each miracle, Jesus was enacting divine authority and reclaiming what had been stolen by evil. Jesus declared that the kingdom of light had come to wipe away sorrow and suffering from sin. But, He would accomplish this task by taking on sorrow and suffering Himself. Though He was innocent, Jesus carried our sins, became a curse, and willingly took the punishment for our crimes against God. Jesus was bruised, beaten, mocked, rejected, and abandoned. As God Himself, Jesus was the chief sufferer because He died for sins He did not commit and experienced the utmost anguish of separation from the Father He perfectly loved. He hung on the cross and suffered a slow death until payment was satisfied, and the redemptive plan was accomplished. When we encounter suffering, we can find comfort in knowing that our Savior suffered for us and understands every hardship we encounter. Even when it feels like it, we are never alone in our pain.

THE LORD IS WITH US IN EVERY
TRIAL; THROUGH EVERY MOMENT
OF SUFFERING, HE CARRIES US.

What does Jesus's *Saving Work* Mean for Sufferers?

Through His life, death, and resurrection from the grave, Jesus saved God's people from sin. We who have put our faith in His saving work are forgiven, and we are credited with Jesus's righteous record. This record means that when God looks at us, He sees the perfection and beauty of Jesus. God welcomes us into His family, and we are redeemed, or bought back, with the love of Jesus. The Holy Spirit dwells inside the faithful followers of Jesus, giving them the comforting and ever-present nearness of God. We no longer walk in darkness, but we are filled with the light of God. We are no longer bound by sin, but by grace through faith, we can worship God and live fully in the way God originally intended. God heals us from the wounds of the past, relieves our suffering in the present, and gives us courage for the future. Day by day, with the help of the Holy Spirit, we are restored from the pollution of sin, and we progressively experience true freedom from darkness.

What does this truth mean for your suffering? In Christ, you can let go of your idols and turn away from their destructive paths. You can overcome the debilitating hold of your addictions. If you are living in poverty or struggling financially, know that Jesus is your eternal treasure. If you fear death or have lost someone, you can have hope that you will live and reunite in eternity with Jesus. If you are mocked, scorned, or shamed, know that God sees you as His beloved child. If you are oppressed by cruel governments or structures, you can be empowered because God's kingdom is stronger and will topple all unjust earthly kingdoms when Jesus returns. If you have been abused physically or if disease is wrecking your body, trust that you will be made whole and new in glory. If you have been abused emotionally or verbally, be assured that there is comfort in a relationship with God because He delights in you and claims you as His own.

The *Good News*

This saving work of Jesus is the good news of the gospel. The gospel is the encouraging and life-changing message of Jesus's life, death, and resurrection, and it equips believers to handle suffering differently from the rest of the world. The gospel is the truth for a weary people, and the story of Scripture moves us to cast our burdens before the cross of Christ. With humility and gratitude, we can resist the attacks of spiritual evil and hold onto our gospel-centered perspective. Though suffering will continue in this fallen world, by the power and grace of God, believers can persevere and hope in the glory to come. We can look forward to when our Savior will come again and finally expel all wickedness. King Jesus will judge the oppressive, cruel, and unjust. He will end all pain and wipe away the tears of sorrow. In His eternal kingdom, suffering will be no more. Until we partake in that paradise, we must share this good news with nonbelievers so they too can have this hope in suffering. Spiritual evil aims to draw people away from God with the hardships of life, but we can point them to the good news of Jesus, declaring a joy worth shouting from the rooftops.

the purpose of suffering

Testimony

The joy we have in Christ can move us to proclaim the Lord's goodness in our lives. Despite the grief around us, the transforming power of the gospel urges us to testify of Christ's work. A testimony is a witness or public declaration of truth. The greatest testimony is declaring the Lordship of Christ and your trust in Him to persevere through life's hardships. In this way, God uses suffering to spread the gospel. The Apostle Paul speaks of the purpose of his suffering in Philippians 1:12-14. While he was unjustly imprisoned, he spoke of God using this circumstance for His glory. Paul writes:

> *Now I want you to know, brothers and sisters, that what has happened to me has actually advanced the gospel, so that it has become known throughout the whole imperial guard, and to everyone else, that my imprisonment is because I am in Christ. Most of the brothers have gained confidence in the Lord from my imprisonment and dare even more to speak the word fearlessly.*

Through the beatings and while in chains, Paul never ceased to testify of the gospel, and in this suffering, God used Paul's words to bring the lost to Him. Paul knew that Christ would be honored in his life and death, so he faced harsh circumstances with joy, courage, and endurance. Similarly, your suffering is not meant for silence. Declare your struggles and your victories in Christ. Cry out, sharing how the saving work of Jesus is giving you hope and strength while you weep over your miscarriage, your job failure, or your depression. People will wonder at the source of your joy. In your testimony, there is much opportunity to help others navigate suffering as you share with them the love of Christ.

"DESPITE THE GRIEF
AROUND US, THE
TRANSFORMING POWER
OF THE GOSPEL
URGES US TO TESTIFY
OF CHRIST'S WORK."

Refinement

Another purpose for suffering is refinement. This type of refinement is not simply the adage, "suffering makes you stronger." Rather, this type of refinement is a sanctification process. Sanctification is the day-by-day transformation in becoming more like Christ. As believers made new by the saving work of Jesus, we strive to overcome the besetting sins of our old self and pursue the image of Christ by the power of the Holy Spirit within us. In this pursuit, we become who we were truly meant to be—people of gentleness, kindness, justice, love, and faith. God uses suffering to bring us closer to the beauty and perfection of Jesus. For instance, in suffering, we are exposed to our idols, our pride, and our limitations. Through these hard moments of recognition, the Holy Spirit brings us to repentance and dependence on God. 1 Peter 1:6-7 states, "You rejoice in this, even though now for a short time, if necessary, you suffer grief in various trials so that the proven character of your faith—more valuable than gold which, though perishable, is refined by fire—may result in praise, glory, and honor at the revelation of Jesus Christ." Peter claims that the product of our suffering—becoming like Jesus—is more valuable than gold. Though suffering can bring out the corruption of sin in our hearts, we can have hope that the Holy Spirit will continue to apply the work of the gospel to us until we are fully refined. One day in eternity with God, we, who will be like brilliant jewels in a king's hand, will stand radiating the glory of Jesus. With no regret, we will look back at the suffering we endured, seeing it all as worth the trouble—for it was in that suffering that we grew and were shaped to more clearly reflect the image of Christ.

Engaging in
Redemptive Work

Seeing the suffering of the world, believers should be moved to engage in redemptive work and bring every sphere under the Lordship of Christ. Corruption, injustice, and insufficient structures are burdens that arouse passions among Christ's ambassadors. As redeemed people, we are called to spread the light, love, and order of God in a dark and chaotic world. By the Holy Spirit, we should use our gifts and positions to manifest the kingdom of God. God has allowed us to witness and experience suffering in order to work for the world's good. As seen in Genesis 1, God designed His world to flourish in His presence. He commissioned Adam and Eve to have dominion — to exercise their God-given authority — over the earth. They were called to steward, or care for, God's creation.

This cultural mandate was fulfilled in Jesus Christ as His resurrecting power realizes true spiritual flourishing and will fully restore the world at His second coming. Since we have the Spirit of Jesus inside us, believers can apply this resurrecting power to all of life, fighting against areas of suffering. For instance, believers can work in medicine to form ethical and restorative practices to counter physical deterioration from sin. Believers can engage in politics to encourage and influence leaders to act with justice and righteousness. We can advocate for the less fortunate and serve the poor. We can serve in public health systems and structures for safer and healthier living. Christian artists can create visual works, music, plays, and films that glorify God. We can volunteer in bleak urban areas to plant greenery and neighborhood gardens that point to the new life we have in Christ. God wants His people to respond to a suffering world. He can lead you to such wonderful, redemptive work for His name's sake.

66

AS REDEEMED PEOPLE, WE ARE CALLED TO
SPREAD THE LIGHT, LOVE, AND ORDER OF GOD
IN A DARK AND CHAOTIC WORLD.

Future Hope

Suffering moves us to long for something better than this fallen world. Throughout our time on earth, we experience continual loss of people and possessions. Like grass withering in intense heat, the things of this life will eventually have their end. Because this world is passing, we must cling to something everlasting: eternity with Jesus. After His death, Christ was raised from the grave. The Father did not leave His obedient Son but resurrected and glorified His body. He ascended to His heavenly throne and will come again to bring the new heavens and earth. King Jesus will usher in the full manifestation of the kingdom of God, and God in all His glory — Father, Son, and Holy Spirit — will dwell among His people. Romans 8:11 states, "And if the Spirit of him who raised Jesus from the dead lives in you, then he who raised Christ from the dead will also bring your mortal bodies to life through his Spirit who lives in you." Like our Savior, we too will resurrect by His power. We will meet Jesus face to face and celebrate our union with Him in a great feast. Our scars will turn into badges of honor and beauty. We will have glorified bodies, praising God forever. Revelation 21:4 tells us, "He will wipe away every tear from their eyes. Death will be no more; grief, crying, and pain will be no more, because the previous things have passed away." In paradise with God, enjoying the goodness of His restored world, we will be in an eternal state of joy, peace, and satisfaction. This truth gives us confident hope when we miss our deceased loved ones or face death ourselves. While suffering loss, we can hope in the truth that death is only temporary and look forward to the day when Christ will raise us to life once again.

PART EIGHT

how to suffer well

Biblical Examples

Read Job 42 and 1 Samuel 1

Voices of suffering are incorporated throughout Scripture. These stories show that God graciously and lovingly makes space for our pain. We can look to these stories to learn how to suffer well. A common theme in them is transparent and vulnerable prayer.

First is Job's story. Job was a man of great wealth, influence, and family. Then one day, all of that disappeared when his estate was stolen, his children tragically died, and his body became inflamed with a severe skin disease. Job wrestled with feelings of abandonment and despair. But, his emotions did not move him to retreat within himself. Instead, they drove him to seek God's face for answers. In Job 10:18-19, Job openly prays, "Why did you bring me out of the womb? I should have died and never been seen. I wish I had never existed but had been carried from the womb to the grave." At the end of the book, by God's grace, Job humbled himself and repented before the Lord.

Hannah is another person who suffered well. She was a woman unable to have children, and for her barrenness, she was mocked and ridiculed. Hannah brought her sorrow to the Lord in prayer. In 1 Samuel 1:11, Hannah prays, "Lord of Armies, if you will take notice of your servant's affliction, remember and not forget me, and give your servant a son, I will give him to the Lord all the days of his life..." Hannah sought the desire of her heart in prayer and dedicated this desire to God.

The greatest example of suffering well is found in Jesus. In the garden of Gethsemane, before He was taken to be crucified, He wept, He mourned, He called out to the Father, "My Father, if it is possible, let this cup pass from me. Yet not as I will, but as you will" (Matthew 26:39). He prayed that His Father would make another way, but this was the only way, and in it, Jesus did not revile—in the lament, in the betrayal and beating, in every part of the suffering and deepest anguish, He gracefully accepted His Father's will so that we could be saved from eternal death and instead spend eternity with Him in glory.

Like these biblical examples, we must practice the discipline of prayer to seek God's help through our suffering. We must also engage in Scripture reading to glean from the people in the faith who came before us. The Old Testament characters can encourage us by their forward hope in Christ's coming. Their stories help us persevere through suffering and look to Jesus's second coming. Additionally, the New Testament believers inspire us by their passion and conviction to spread the gospel. Their movement urges us to hold to our faith, even in the darkest moments.

Walking
with Others

In the body of Christ, one never suffers alone. However great the temptation to pull away from others in your hurt or struggle—to keep to yourself in shame or fear—believers are called to be in deep community with one another. Pray for the courage to reach out to people within your local gospel-affirming and Bible-centered church. This community embodies and reflects the love and relational nature of God. 1 Corinthians 12:26 tells us that as the body of Christ, "if one member suffers, all the members suffer with it; if one member is honored, all the members rejoice with it." As we go through life together, we share in the joys and pains of life. We bear each other's burdens and lighten the load that suffering brings.

In the same way that our community walks with us through struggles we may face, so we should be present for others in their times of need. As we seek to serve those we meet, we listen to their stories of grief and express vulnerability when sharing our stories with them as well. Often, the Lord allows us to use our own experiences with pain and suffering as a way to more closely relate with another or offer encouragement in a way that others cannot. We can be encouraged by the spiritual journeys of fellow brothers and sisters in Christ as our friends persevere alongside us and we alongside them. Commit to the church, and surround yourself with the people of God. Through community together, we can demonstrate the transforming power of the gospel and the love of God that overcomes all suffering.

IN THE BODY OF CHRIST,
ONE NEVER SUFFERS ALONE.

"OFTEN, THE LORD
ALLOWS US TO USE
OUR OWN EXPERIENCES
WITH PAIN AND SUFFERING
AS A WAY TO MORE
CLOSELY RELATE WITH
ANOTHER OR OFFER
ENCOURAGEMENT IN A WAY
THAT OTHERS CANNOT."

Thank you for studying
God's Word with us!

CONNECT WITH US
@thedailygraceco
@kristinschmucker

CONTACT US
info@thedailygraceco.com

SHARE
#thedailygraceco
#lampandlight

VISIT US ONLINE
thedailygraceco.com

MORE DAILY GRACE
The Daily Grace App
Daily Grace Podcast